MIRRORS

A Collection of Poetry

DENNIS J. GAYLE

Copyright © 2023 Dennis J. Gayle.

All rights reserved. No part of this book may be reproduced, stored, or transmitted by any means—whether auditory, graphic, mechanical, or electronic—without written permission of both publisher and author, except in the case of brief excerpts used in critical articles and reviews. Unauthorized reproduction of any part of this work is illegal and is punishable by law.

ISBN: 979-8-88640-005-2 (sc)
ISBN: 979-8-88640-006-9 (hc)
ISBN: 979-8-89031-545-8 (e)

Because of the dynamic nature of the Internet, any web addresses or links contained in this book may have changed since publication and may no longer be valid. The views expressed in this work are solely those of the author and do not necessarily reflect the views of the publisher, and the publisher hereby disclaims any responsibility for them.

One Galleria Blvd., Suite 1900, Metairie, LA 70001
(504) 702-6708
1-888-421-2397

CONTENTS

LEAVES 1
MOUNT SAKURAJIMA 2
UMGENI RIVER BIRD PARK 3
KOOLOONBUNG CREEK NATURE RESERVE 4
SUZHOU GARDENS 5
MAGNOLIA MEDITATION 6
LETTUCE GARDEN 7
ORCHIDS 8
ON THE BEACH 9
ALEXANDRA PARK 10
ANDRÉ 11
SOPHIA 12
ASH WEDNESDAY 13
ATTITUDES 14
AU REVOIR 15
CALIFORNIA CHRISTMAS 16
OCHO RIOS ROUNDABOUT 17
CARIBBEAN WAVES 18
LOCH NESS 19
FRANGIPANI 20
CHAMPS ELYSSEES 21
SQUIRRELS 22
COUNTRY MATTERS 23
DIE BLAU KIRCHE 24
PONTE VEDRA BEACH 25
GARE DES INVALIDES 26
GOOD FRIDAY, ST. THOMAS 27
AVRIL PATRICIA 28
DERRY HUGH 29
HYDE PARK MORNING 30

INVERTED FOUNTAIN	31
HURRICANE SEASON	32
BOUGAINVILLEA SONG	33
JE REGRETTE	34
KINGSTON	35
LA MER	36
LAST TANGO IN MARBLE ARCH	37
LONDON EVENING	38
LOUGH	39
LOVE	40
NEW YEAR	41
NEW YORK	42
NOCTURNE	43
OPPORTUNITY COST	44
PAPER TIGER	45
PONT DU LAUSANNE	46
PORT HENDERSON	47
RAINBOW'S END	48
REVERIE	49
GANGES SUNSET	50
LOVERS	51
THE HARDER THEY COME	52
THE LESSON	53
THE OBSERVER	54
TIME	55
VIGIL	56
VISIT TO THE LOUVRE	57
WORDS	58
YOURS FAITHFULLY	59
BIRDS	60
APPROACHING THE ACROPOLIS	61
MORNING GLORY	62
MIRRORS	63
PALE BLUE DOT	64

LEAVES

Emerald-green leaves,
Drinking sunlight.
Delicate cupped hands,
Awaiting dew blessings.
Breathing, moss-green
Leaves, stomata flaring
In passing gusts.
Elegant olive-green
Leaves swaying in the wind,
Dancing the long day.
Forest bathing, *shrinrin-yoku*,
Lime-green leaves, all
A-quiver in the breeze.
Transpiring, aqua-green
Leaves, reversed with dark,
Recreating air. Starlit,
Pine-green leaves,
Cloaking the still night,
In quietly eloquent speech.
Tea-green leaves drawing
Questing eyes, sharing
Translucent shade. Veined,
Fern-green undersides –
Lymphatic nodes,
Carrying chlorophyll,
Channeling life's contours.

MOUNT SAKURAJIMA

Kagoshima dawn,
Sunlight splashes
Mount Sakurajima.
Ash-decorated streets,
Wisps of weary caldera-
Offered smoke.
Pink-white rhododendrons
On Satsuma and Osumi
Girdle Kagoshima Bay.
An occasional rumble
Above a laurel tree walk,
Market stalls with green
Daikon radishes
Accent the scene.
A way of seeing
Is a way of not seeing.
Salarymen stream the
Street below, where
Women with exquisite
Pink silk parasols
Ward off drifting ashes.
Sunlight spears
Sakurajima's valleys,
Raw anomie blooms.
Not knowing
What is unknown, yet
Stretching for the light.
We're all ashes in the winds
Of this warm Kagoshima dawn.

UMGENI RIVER BIRD PARK

Waterfalls and aviaries,
Flowing river beyond.
Salt-laden air from
Durban's Indian Ocean
Flows through the lungs.
Sharp-taloned, silent owls.
Long-legged brown cranes
Fly, necks outstretched.
Bright yellow-beaked hornbills,
Long-tailed macaws,
All blue and white.
Laughing brown kookaburras.
Beige-beaked toucans,
Stern, black-coated vultures,
All wheeling in flight.
A rainbow of spectators,
Indian, Zulu, White.
Memories flood.
Hard sugarcane joints
Always sweetest.
Who beats a drum
With one finger?
Roaring lions
Kill no one.
A crocodile's strength
Remains in the water.
Oh, wizened and wise
Dalitso, who spoke
Such simple truths,
And now can speak no more.

KOOLOONBUNG CREEK NATURE RESERVE

A sturdy, weathered
Kooloonbung boardwalk.
Stands of corkwood trees,
Shadowed in sunlight.
Limbs curving gracefully
Over still creek water.
Lead-hued lizards dart,
Red flying foxes shelter
In Casuarina tree boughs.
Yellow butterflies swirl,
Grass rippled by lazy breezes.
Gray, white-chested koalas
Perch in eucalyptus trees,
Baby mammals held close.
Coffee-colored kangaroos,
Ears alert in rest,
Powerful tails reserved.
Mangroves slowly spread,
A cool, greening peace.
Cemetery of settlers,
Elegant carved tombstones,
Fenced sanctuaries,
Eloquent in silence.
Ancient Gondwana trees.
Didgeridoos shrill sonorously
Across sixty thousand years.
Aboriginal Dreaming,
Sacred *Tijurunga* paintings
On flat stone canvases. Saurian
Water Dragon lies in wait.

SUZHOU GARDENS

Water lilies floating,
Scarlet and cream Koi
Fish idling, jade-green lake.
White cirrostratus clouds,
Floating lazily overhead.
The arcs of carved roofs,
With bright yellow highlights,
All a-curving to the sky.
Red paper lanterns lit
Haunting ancestral temples,
On Shantang Street.
Tiger Hill Pagoda,
Leaning against the borne
Weight of centuries.
Trimmed Bonsai trees,
Mirror green generations
Of master gardeners.
Marco Polo came,
Saw and learned
Ways of silk and steel.
By changing attitudes
Towards experiences,
Each issue considered,
Irremediably altered.
Ubiquitous calligraphy,
Hanzi characters.
Compound logograms,
Uniting blazing sun,
Moon's chilled splendor,
Mother Earth and Father Sky.

MAGNOLIA MEDITATION

Watching the clouds scud light across the sky,
Sunlight and shadow stream through rippling grass.
Spreading Magnolia branches elicit a sigh,
New flower's fresh cream is all too swift to pass.
Yet phalanges of roots explore the fertile earth,
Tree speaks to tree, in languages unheard.
Years come and go, shadowed by tree ring's girth,
Blossoms deftly pollinated by tweeting bird.
Human arteries mirror Magnolia capillaries,
But birth, not life, yet counters death's desires.
Mitochondrial Eve, generational curtsies.
Green grass and trees still beckon all our eyes.
Negative with positive entropies entwined.
An arboreal bloom flowers, another dies.

LETTUCE GARDEN

Sleep's lusty restoration births anew
Vistas of possibility and rebuffed pain.
Wise and wary pessimists conserve the view
Rain never inundates a dust bowl plain.
Unflagging believers in what can be seen
Regularly observe only what is believed.
The obscure mysteries of last night's dream
Often unconsciously mirrored and re-conceived.
Minutes inexorably multiply into militant hours,
Life's days are ever done when least expected.
In navigating between flamboyant showers
Of opportunities, sometimes orchestrated,
Obstacles bespeak the best paths unseeded.
Trenchant aphids, lettuce garden desiccated.

ORCHIDS

Warm yellow greeting,
Uplifted anthers
Meet the day.
Multivariant roots
Engage earth and air.
Vigorous green leaves
Dreaming of tomorrow.
Nothing is lasting,
Everything renewed.
Successive forgetting.
Appreciated acceptance,
Unique understanding.
Petals like purple flags
Pistils splashed white,
In a delicate dance.
A river of orchid joy,
As evening approaches.

ON THE BEACH

This morning, I thrilled to hearing the
Fresh-wet, cool earth's song
While a chorus of blue jays and thrushes
Sparkled in my ears, a heady wine stain.
I saw how the dew-tipped red roses bloomed
Heart-high in my lush green garden,
Saw too their concealed thorns,
Yet could not feel their hurt.

Then this noon, the road rode white and
Dusty behind, all of a-curve over the dry hills,
In the heat and clarity of the all-creating,
All-devouring sun. I had ceased to desire another
Drink than pure, cold water, though love's knowledge
Lingered on the lips. Now and again, a thunder of sighs
Rolled around me, and in their midst,
I trembled to hear my own.

Now, this still evening, I'm tasting the first wafts
Of a tangy sea breeze, while the strange stars above
Sparkly dimly, forlornly. I walk out across the
Moon-bleached sand of the curving beach,
Listening anxiously. From another place and time,
Receding notes of a wildly sad yet brilliantly gay fado
Float out to meet the silence of the onrushing night.

ALEXANDRA PARK

It is not that the light-tipped blue of evening
Merges coolly into the cotton puff insubstantiality
Of the delicate, beech-leaved framed stretches of sky,
Hanging loosely overhead.

It is not that the echoes of boyish bicycle-borne
Laughter rebound that much more swiftly now, from the
Stippled green of the ever more distant hills.

It is not that in the incautious eye of the mind,
Fireflies still flicker, littering the trail of the
Gathering future with the poignant, personal evanescence
Of the kaleidoscopic, yet stubbornly immutable past.

Rather, each breeze-bent, fragile blade of grass bows
Yet again more gracefully, reluctant to depart the
Stage of the retiring day, incredulous of the hard,
Fresh strength of the morning, tickling my extended feet
Persistently – and then at last, tiring of a vain protest,
Yields with a wisdom born of comprehended experience,
Melts into the dim interstices of the silence from which it came.

ANDRÉ

You never wanted to go to bed at night, then.
Your blue pajamas, an unwished-for signal.

Sometimes, I could almost touch the intensity
Of your joy for jumping, the passion, the excitement,
Rising and falling. But the real challenge was to gauge
The self-conscious freedom of that morning push
On the bedroom door, to fix the reflections that
Sparkled in the windows of your brown eyes, as the
Sparrows chirped in the poplar trees outside. How many
Unasked questions hung there then, in the branches
Of your mind, leaves unwilling to be whirled away?

You were a ratoon of four years standing, and
I watched you taste the wetness of the London rain.

SOPHIA

Fresh brown eyes.
A merry, lilting smile,
Thoughtful trust.
Daddy, do you want to watch this?
Lithe little socked feet,
Padding on the beige carpet
Flee myriads of monsters
In your violet dreams.
A yellow-tailed rainbow pony.
Big Bird on Sesame Street.
Disneyworld's Easter Parade.
But true bliss is a wide swing
In an alamander Florida sunset.
A four-year old fountain of youth,
A dream fulfilled.

ASH WEDNESDAY

Today, an unsure, lingering look
Across the teeming centuries.
Your eyes meet mine.
I almost turn away.
A leap of faith,
The long, dark night in wait.
What were the ways
That led me here?
Atoms scattered from stars,
A universe seething with
Dark matter, black holes,
Colliding constellations
In cold, interstellar space.
But the vice of time
Will not release the gaze.
To breathe is to choose.
I so much want to echo
"Lord, I believe,
Help Thou mine unbelief!"

ATTITUDES

Joy best understands sorrow,
Anxiety, peace; loneliness, companionship.
Without sustaining deep friendship,
Passion fades. My love and I speak,
Or enjoy each other in silence.
Partners who bring light to our lives
Constitute life's true riches –
Not financial assets or wealth.
Let's always leave each other
With hugs and loving words.
It may be for the last time.
The people we care about most
Must often depart too soon.
I know we'll remember that
Anger never justifies cruelty;
From an act of an instant
Heartaches for life.
We can see in a situation
Quite different scenarios.
Argument coexists with love;
Apparent agreement may be mistaken.
Sometimes, we must learn to forgive ourselves.
Background and circumstance influence our being,
But we are accountable for whom we become.

AU REVOIR

You, my love, new purpose tenderness,
A-thrill on the subway's penitential seat.
Warm eyes, a year of uncoupled tension,
And time become a tautness
That cannot be denied
In an eternity of prolix sophistries.
Yet still a space for wonder,
If not for truth, drowned
In the rattling of a moment's wheels.
Too zealously dramatic. I will not cry,
Though all my heart's dry blood is holding still.

CALIFORNIA CHRISTMAS

Continual exchanges of benign greetings,
Tinged with gold sunlight, red poinsettias.
Sententious city hucksters sum profit and loss.
Timeless rumors of war, hymns of peace.
A tumble of children laughing in the streets.
A man without the inner glow of myth
Walks coatless in the coming winter rain.
To give is to grow; not the inertia of custom
Nor a narrow calculation entirely dims
These traded blessings of gratitude.
Relaxation is the wisdom of letting go,
As time shadows all, and slows this pen.
A moment's silence frees the gaze to rest
On the fantastic flowering
Of a cold December Crown of Thorns.

OCHO RIOS ROUNDABOUT

Old couple, rough wooden handcart,
Across the street, a million moods away.
Star apples served on sunlight,
To ease the strain up the slope.

Eyes holding yesterday's yielding
Almost bless the squeak of the wheels.
Showers of sweat cloud the view.
Another market day, another corner.

Late rush hour, there's no
Time for such wide smiles,
Dimmed in the throbbing minutes
Of my red blood, of my uneven engine.

CARIBBEAN WAVES

Always surging, never stopping.
Always surging, never stopping.
Iridescent, breathtakingly delicate
Bubbles born of sun-flecked, pure white froth
That danced merrily over the blue-green depths,
That sped on swiftly towards the shore,
To burst, with an almost audible sigh
In the light of remote, enigmatic stars.
Always surging, never stopping.
Always surging, never stopping.
Tacking gracefully at the breath of the wind,
Merging, separating, clashing, fleeing,
A myriad rainbow shades,
The ultimate color of wonder,
A symmetry of wild, aching discord,
That swirled for the space of a vibrant chord,
That died in the clash of the stern chorale!

LOCH NESS

Cirrocumulus clouds reflected in water,
Boat engine breaching the brooding silence.
A Union Jack's blood-red backdrop in winter,
The deck's steel guardrails yet ambivalent.
Green moors rise gently from the shores,
Reaching into the icy-dark skies above.
The indifferent waters of the loch lap
Against the curve of the cove.
Questing imaginations scour and slap
Away folktales and chimeras arising
From the unplumbed depths of time.
Past disappeared, present fleeting,
Into still unshaped futures dreaming.
Remote mitochondrial memories abiding.

FRANGIPANI

Purple bougainvillea ablaze in the afternoon sun.
White, yellow-tinged frangipani flowers,
Welcome breezes of blessings at Whitsun.
Night falls suddenly in a spate of showers.
A horde of frangipani worms will swarm
These delicate green leaves by tomorrow.
Such deciduous plumeria shrubs warm
Human hearts, but bring prospective sorrow.
Advancing phalanxes of green worms, bright
Black stripes and busy mouths in sallies,
That race the honey bee's darting flight,
Full ardent sphinx moth caterpillar bellies.
A tentative hand moves to remove a pest,
Arrested by pointed horn tails, raised in delight.

CHAMPS ELYSSEES

You didn't really think it would change anything
Did you? But impatient fingers run on ahead.
Let me tell you what it was actually like
In a rain of nerves below Etoile.
Sidewalk crowds, hazy sunshine.
A Valentino movie, with
Camel questions, charades of sand
An uncompleted dance.
Later, a warming café au lait,
White-gloved waiters hurrying by.
Yet the theatre within's absurd,
A *danse macabre*, in blue shadows.
Reflections chill the air.
The steadily approaching
Place de la Concord
Promises nothing.
But it doesn't matter at all, my dear.
How could it,
Our own oasis suddenly in sight?

SQUIRRELS

Squirrels sailing across wind-rocked tree limbs,
Bright eyes, twitching tails, momentary rest.
Sinuous grey squirrels leaping light across
Graceful green magnolia leaves at dusk.
White-chested squirrels, whiskers twitching,
Dancing through cream-flowered dogwood trees,
As altostratus clouds drift in the lavender sky.
Changing the ways in which we gaze at squirrels
Can change perspectives on human life,
Lived forwards, but understood backwards.
Squirrels rippling light across the emerald grass,
Racing with the soughing of the breeze.
One squirrel chases another charmingly
Up the smooth, fawn trunk of a primrose tree.
A lissome squirrel in flight lands on a slender,
Shaking twig, regains an improbable balance,
And soars, toes spread, to a stouter bough.

COUNTRY MATTERS

Granny, slow
In a rocking chair.
Verandah overlooks an entropy of sand.
Antique, horn-fenced spectacles
Magnify a strutting rooster's comb.
Cumulus clouds, "*doctor*" breeze,
Passing patters of dreary rain.
A parade of bright yellow chickens
Cheeping cheerfully near the pond.
The rise and fall of the heavy sea.
Trail of smoke from a bush fire,
A bull-like bellow down the road.
Granny low,
In a mocking chair.

DIE BLAU KIRCHE

Slowly, I enter the blue shadows.
Echoes of stained-glass windows
Surround me, and silence gathers.
The pull of an old wooden cross
Beyond the serried, worn pews.
I cannot turn away.
A soar of baroque arches above
Draws my wondering gaze.
The world is shot with light.
I forget to breathe.
A diastolic glow of love
Exploding in the heart,
Drums of primordial time
Pounding in the arteries.
An ocean of longing
Sweeping through the veins.
Mandalas of melody
Caressing my soul.
Marches of mirrored samsaras
Beckoning within.
Incinerated uncertainties,
Routed by the light.
My assembled atoms sing
Of the stars from which they came.
I am the turmoil of all humanity,
In a moment's ocean of belonging.
An ardent prayer pervades my being,
Pulsing through my pores,
In undulating waves.
Silently, I leave the blue shadows,
Eyes wet with wonder.

PONTE VEDRA BEACH

Seven low piles in the low-tide distance,
Stretching through the swelling sea
To the burnt sienna sand flats.
Bare feet sinking in the velvety sand,
As we pass shrouds of rigid jelly fish,
And protected logwood turtle nests.
Looking out to the dark horizon,
Where a naval frigate slips from sight,
Walkers and runners pass, eying each other.
If human eyes saw souls through bodies
Sunlight would shimmer in different ways.
Altocumulus clouds sail through blue skies,
Above restless tidal pools that surface
As whirling tides of thoughts go out.
Swimmers in black wet suits surf the sea,
As green grass straggles fringe the sand,
Obstacles and paths to the gathering future.
Each effort-full step slowly recreating
Experiences yet unknown, if partially
Remembered in the salty mists of time.

GARE DES INVALIDES

It usually seems so much easier
To climb four steps at a time.
A deliberate stretch
Out of the seductive depths of the Metro,
Than to adopt the unsteadily measured pace
Of that arthritic Algerian waiter, shoulders
Huddled against the slow-unfolding December dawn.
But there's a stranger in the skin today,
Afraid to step out on the floodlit stage.
To discard the complaisant shield
Of a comfortably neutral apartment,
Where words invest the elliptical lampshade
Precisely, in irresistible formations,
Nothing lost, and nothing gained.
Outside, it is raining again.
Will it matter tomorrow
Whether or not I proceed?

GOOD FRIDAY, ST. THOMAS

Drums of time, slow pounding in the arteries,
A prayer of rain, ignorant brown earth,
Waiting to yield, in a dream of creation.
Caress of warm sand, surge of a turquoise wave.
Tomorrow's misted symphony, uncaring ears.
Dazzle of sun through the trees, widened eyes.
A ceaseless march of foam in the wind, with
A stormy dance of fragile yellow butterflies.
I cannot bear the salt taste of your grave,
Trusting gaze. Limping words form a maze
Of innumerate fences; headlights in the dark.
Drums of time, subsiding through the veins.

AVRIL PATRICIA

Our father's lovely, auburn-hairéd girl,
She lashed by love left school in flight.
Now combing Teneshia's hair into a curl,
A caring mother halting children's fight.
Kind bespectacled black eyes, wide smile,
Nurse and Bishop seeking ways to serve,
Dry sense of humor seasoning her style.
Now a grandmother, counting life's curve,
As greying hairs signal passing years.
Revered Elder, ministering to her flock,
Acute sensitivity to human tears,
Celebrating the truths of life's bedrock.
Forlorn fight for survival of the flesh,
Yet grace to counter mutant dread disease.

DERRY HUGH

A dimpled cheek with captivating smiles,
Supported by persuasive patters of talk.
A life spent in tormented action, traveling miles,
Jaunty-capped on a Coney Island boardwalk,
Itinerant repairman, salesman, dreaming of flight.
Such generous, kind eyes counter vengeful rage,
Island memories clouded in limnéd light.
Warm impulses of love, yet restless marriage,
Cigarettes and beer, blue Miami seascapes,
Seeking to obliterate unwanted inner sights,
Roaming across dark and dreary landscapes,
Visions of automobile freeways, liberty nights,
Philadelphia dreams dissolving into ashes.
Irrepressible spirit, searching for his crest,
Still smiling and joking amid interior clashes.
Restless soul, passion spent, final peaceful rest.

HYDE PARK MORNING

Heathrow arrival,
Kind indifference,
Snow without,
And eyes within.
Season tickets,
Tube life, unsmiling.
Another stranger to
Make the scene.
Rush hour work,
Pounds in hand,
Cups of tea.
Pub glasses clink,
Red buses groan.
Oval sidewalk,
Amber streetlights.
It's a Hyde Park morning,
Brooding Victory.
Old overcoat,
Imported dream.

INVERTED FOUNTAIN

California dreaming, a girl in a cage.
So, you really like Evita?
Purpose, a wild, unanswered question.
Which you weren't going to ask, anyway.
Instinct searches for a cave,
As the night of a thousand stars
Recedes into contemplation.
The lengthening shadows
Form inchoate threats to scythe
The green grass of reason,
Stretching ever more languorously now
Across a perversity of pampas.
The inverted fountain at our feet
Splashes strange, sad stories.
Evanescent emotions shimmer
Down a carved rush of stones.

HURRICANE SEASON

Jamaica, the sun a shapely fire, from the
Cool of an elegant beachside villa.
Dazzling white paper, pale blue words
Flung to net a five o' clock evening.
Tall coconut trees erect long shadow
Signposts, all a -shuddering in the wind.
Sharp gusts, lolling green bamboos
And a crossing of parched Poinciana.
A violent thunderstorm rocks the heart.
And you, light years away,
Table of insouciant ignorance
Set for two. Tomorrow's sorrow
Smolders in your eyes.

BOUGAINVILLEA SONG

Scarlet joy dances with yellow delights,
Purple pirouettes with red highlights.
Orange petals shimmer in the breeze,
Delicately veined triple petals seize
Our gaze. while anther eyes tease.
A pretty pink florescence catches
Gentle morning sunlight matches
Magenta bougainvillea snatches
Attention with a trilled rubato.
Lovely blue-tinged sfumato,
Variegated bougainvillea animato.
Trumpets of tea bougainvillea
Climb trellises above pink azalea,
Fluting delight to our creamy dahlia,
Lying in a bed of plush pink peonies.

JE REGRETTE

It is odd that a stand of purple jacaranda
Opens such an elegiac inner passage.
Time is a frame for an existential river,
A seethe of sudden rapids round the bend.
Once dear faces, places, ineluctably dismissed dreams….
That sun-distant, hay-stacked field, and a
Laughing boy, ever running free.
A murmur of promises, a sensual shrug,
The curve of an elegant leg on the Rue Midi.
Wind song, effortless rush on the edge
Of the endless freeway.
To arrive is to grow unaccountably sad
For the insistent scent of an old and faded flower.

KINGSTON

And once again yellow poui trees
Send shivers of scarlet delight
Along the limbs of the poinciana.
A cool August breeze restlessly
Sweeps the grass to their knees
In a sun-washed shimmer.
A little cloud of swaying buttercups
Laughs on the Kingston sidewalk.
Yet your will is like a barefoot boy,
Hands outstretched at the traffic light.
And once again a dangerous pity
Poisons my waking dreams.
I shall remember you, most of all,
Lying on the floor,
The restless light of battle in your eyes.

LA MER

A smooth of
Undulating sapphire ripples
Vein a patient palette,
A sleight of calm.
Cloud shadow ink blots below,
Azure skies above.
Elongated memories
Beckon in silence.
Green islands
Inhabit my being.
Harbors curve
Horizons of doubt.
Home is the hunt for
Shards of certitude.
Orpheus would earn the
Slow peace of acceptance,
Warm blessings of sunlight.
Each day's anxieties drift
Into elegant cumuli.
A shared evening zephyr,
A touch of understanding.
Aphrodite smiles
As the moon rides high.

LAST TANGO IN MARBLE ARCH

Blue moon beams falling softly on the mind,
A hundred days, a hundred years ago.
Felt integers of action, natural, whole,
An emphasis on old, ecdysiast dreams.
The distant rumbling of restless rocks,
Whimpers of survival in the raw streets.
Dry gold-brown leaves, a flurry in the park.
A black cat on a long, lamplit lane,
With darkened houses and smoking chimneys.
Tango of smooth water, soft-splashing slowly
From the still, green dolphins on the
Street corner fountain. But there's a
Blizzard of dust and paper all
Dancing in the heart.
Uncomprehending eyes, a wish to sleep.

LONDON EVENING

The seasons change.
I too.
And cannot but be one with that wide cry
Wheeling from the black outstretched arms
Beyond my window
To the impeccably cold grey above.
The tears of strange centuries have whirled
Past my feet, near Westminster,
While the same bird songs that Homer heard
Have warmed my heart.
I have no calipers, and cannot measure time;
Only vague memories of a prolonged forgetting.
The seasons change.
I too,
There are days when the blood runs bright,
Air tastes as fresh as though
No one had ever drunk this life before.
Streetlights sparkle, lending sudden magic
To both Embankments, to the bridge itself.
As the anxious, enwrapped crowd hurries past.
The river reflects the brightness
On its now more somber surface.
The seasons change.
I too.

LOUGH

Dark water, planning smoothly into light-stippled ripples,
Unresting questions skein, infused with etiolated shadows.
Wind teasing the rushes, old-fashioned acolytes,
Undated genuflections, a solipsistic altar.
Words written on the ebb and flow of the lough,
Evening burning steadily into night.

Dark water, framing self-possessed wavelets,
A fleeting signpost seeks an oblique fate
Across a colloquy of unplanned dimensions.
A passing fancy, a moment's commitment.
Rowing boats by the decayed boathouse,
There's a lone oar floating on across the lake.

LOVE

Love is a verb that soars
Beyond rational thought,
Brooking no boundaries,
Always reaching towards the Light.
Love is a flash of lightening,
Rippling through the Soul.
Love is an immanent hunger
For the quiet of completion.
Love surrenders to need
For the recurrent joys of merger.
Love desires to bring
Contentment to each beloved.
Love is an immanent peace,
Recreating Gardens of Eden.
Love's a long meditation upon our
Blessings from the Creator.
Love is a passion of mind that can
Glow ever brighter through time.
Love is the breath of life,
A caring without ending.
Love is the magic of touch,
That soothes away all tears.
Love is a verb that soars
Beyond rational thought.

NEW YEAR

You know it's not going to make any difference
Don't you? Yet if you insist, I will
Try once again to map a way
Between yesterday's ramshackle stairs
And the gentle, determinate swirl
Of those maple leaves,
In flight all Indian summer.
An impersonal payment is never enough,
As Rodin's Walking Man
Keeps striding onwards
In compressed muscles of feet.
There are so many crippled resolutions
In this City of the Angels.
Aged and unlovely winter leaves,
All curled and torn at the edges,
Awaiting a wind to blow them away.
Perhaps you were right, after all.

NEW YORK

Tightrope walk of washing
Strung out against a fire-scaped sky.
A reach of twin towers out on Manhattan.
The crumpled wino sprawled quite naturally,
Only a sidewalk away. New York!
I walk your streets with love and despair,
All a-tugging at the sleeves, Everyman,
Any day. Subway-tamed faces pulled tight
Against the dark. A farrago of accents,
A hundred tones, awaiting in unattended
Tension that lucky break, an elusive dream.
Almost forgot, shoes pinching on the feet,
Prospect Park, Fall melody of roses,
Not quite instant news on Times Square.
Your suspended breath, widened eyes,
Poised precariously between past and future,
Under fifty-five degrees of clear skies,
All those ladders to climb, those bills to pay!

NOCTURNE

Each day is a completed journey
Woven unsteadily into the warp
And woof of tenuous memories.
Rain and sunshine counterpoint
Recollected sorrow and laughter.
The poise of learned patience,
All too readily shattered.
Inchoate reflections roam
Fractals of consciousness,
Tomorrow is an unborn child,
Faith, a silver flicker of angel fish.
Late on the edge of a constrained night,
The ambition of the last glowing embers
In the slumbering, wrought-iron fireplace
Is to not be put out, defying the dark.

OPPORTUNITY COST

Wind swishing through the pines,
An échelon of echoes in the mirror.
The smile of Tovine's Spanish Gipsy Boy,
Fixed, eternal. To you, I reach out
Warm fingers of thought
In the damp cradle of morning.
A litany of raindrops on the blinds,
Gathering to a rattling rage on the roof.
Bare-legged children shouting in the street;
A paper boat poised cockily in the
Currents of a turbulent gutter.
Tomorrow may be different, you believe.

PAPER TIGER

A stretching of misty streets outside,
Precariously hung curtains on the mind.
The Tree of Fortune slowly greens,
A shaft of sunlight lengthens on the wall.
Each ingot, weighed within the hand,
Imperfect crucible, misrepresents
Construed position on the chessboard's plane.
I lose your words and
Lose the sound of laughter,
Yet hesitate to judge the moment ripe,
And doubt the mirror's evanescent taste.
Yet still the hourglass looms
More monstrous and more tall,
Each grain of sand become a trumpet blast.
The dream of sunlight fades, and leaves me blind.

PONT DU LAUSANNE

Bridge on the night Rhone,
Bright slivers of reflections probe the mind.
Time did not flow in ordered, conscious moments.
It fled, like grains of sand slipping from the hand
Which led
Back to the sea-lashed shore
From whence they came.
Wide lake of Geneva,
Lapping green questions on the quay
Near Calvin's frozen stone.
A lake-refracted, fleeting half-moon
Holds the endless pulsing of the blood.
Dark voices murmur behind,
Echoes of calculating eyes within.
Bridge on the deep Rhone,
Carillon of distant bells, starlit sky.

PORT HENDERSON

Sapphire sea beyond the bar,
Lone dog sniffing slowly down the beach.
Boats sprawl on the sand, unready for flight.
November rain, a huddling of mangroves.
So many waiting caves upon the cliff,
Footprints that never seemed to change, to end.

Shadow of a vulture overhead,
Black fishermen, net stretched for mending.
Free-floating laughter from around the point,
Hot blue sky, touched with cactus.
Coach idling, steam rising from the road,
School children running light along the shore.

RAINBOW'S END

There's another stranger
Clutching at the root
Of the standard deviation.
Echoes answer questions
That fall softly mute,
Under cream cirrus clouds,
Black, imponderably starlit sky.
There's a despairing winter visitor
Knocking at the old church door,
Thinking herself all too late.
Dense forests of patient hands
Vainly extended through fenced,
Overgrown trails through
Farragoes of self-sustaining fears.
Daunting tangles of scar tissue
Clog the hearts, whose eyes
Wear heavy, bureaucratic masks.
Kindness withers in the freezing rain.

REVERIE

Praise is at best a wish,
Or a faintly mirrored willingness,
Ending often in a wistful regret,
Mourning what the sun had no will to shine on.

Feverishly, yet I forge
On the molten altar of human desire,
Racked similes, that fade away
Before my grasp can firm them.

Innocent actress, undifferentiated stages,
An adagio of inchoate ideograms, inflamed
With the warming glow of a rosebud petal
In the incandescence of early morning.

Gold earrings sparkle in sunlight,
Angry shake of the head.
Laughter, and sudden sea breezes.
Waves fret, intently, pensive. And so
I paint word pictures on this tanned, living sand!

GANGES SUNSET

In a sudden hush,
Soft, etiolated shadows sketch the sky.
A sinuous road stretches down
To a flight of scattered egrets.
An adagio of cowbells,
Swollen, sun-kissed cumulus clouds.
A sutra of susurrating voices,
As men bathe in the Ganges below.
Saffron and cinnamon scent the air,
Far from New Delhi's hectic heat,
As the sea beyond shapes sultry dreams.
The approaching monsoon murmurs,
In the wary green mountains behind,
As shards of driftwood splinter in the sky.

LOVERS

Seeking to give exquisite joy,
One to another, body and spirit.
Exchanging the most
Primal and ethereal
Forms and flows of love.
Hugging each other,
Making breakfast bakes,
Watching sunrises sunset.
Walking hand in hand through
Life's valleys, presaged
By fear, sorrow and pain.
Yet sharing freely in all
Touching our hearts.
Continually consulting
Soaring hopes and dreams.
Gently singing a moment's
Forgotten soul song back.
Arms and legs closely
Wrapped in passion.
Heads bent in prayer,
For dreamt tomorrows.
Doubts almost dispelled,
Tentative tributaries of joy
Seek an imagined delta.

THE HARDER THEY COME

A cigarette lies smoking in the wind,
Whitened spar in the black street.
A pile of broken bottles stuns the eye,
Semaphore by the blind wooden steps.
Banana peelings clutch the midday shadows,
Bronze tap cranes the neck across the yard.
The splattering of water in a marooned cistern
Leavens the lusty buzzing of the flies,
Punctuated by the creaking of the gate.
A blessing of church bells loops across the sky.
Police patrol car screeches down the road;
A scatter of sparks and ashes in the breeze.

THE LESSON

Ink-black words,
On crisp cream paper.
Curiosity shapes a self-portrait
In the critical mirror of time.
With Rembrandt's Night Watchmen,
Looking beyond fractal edges of light.
Ineluctably, a way of seeing
Remains a way of not seeing.
Night spins a childhood fairyland anew,
On the shadowed hill across the street.
Spider webs shimmer in
Dewdrops, all green and gold.
The vibrant dance of the seven veils
Mimics morning's memory.
Yet tenuous hope unfolds,
In a morning glory's song,
As I learn again
To applaud or accept each moment,
Whether recorded
By the pulsing digits of my watch, or not.

THE OBSERVER

A day is the art of the possible,
Fraying tapestry, for the occasional
Incurious glance, in the bitter familiarity
Of my unknown country.
Today, I set the warm, greedy clarity
In a baby's eyes against a walk
Of wary, wounded and lonely people.
Where do they all come from?
There are too many gunmen in my dreams,
Butt and nozzle merging into one.
That old man on the corner's
Lost his way. Will this schoolboy,
Stone in hand, help him to find it?
The observer stands condemned,
Unable to avoid his own choices.

TIME

did not flow
in ordered, conscious moments.
It fled,
Sand grains slipping through
Unwilling hands,
Back to the sea-lashed shores
From whence they came –
Save for those moments
That still breathe anew,
Bathed, each one
In poignant tremors
Of joy, sorrow, or pain.
Memory's directors edit
Remote places and roles.
Years, months and days,
Subsumed by sensibilities.
Wrinkles, aches and pains –
Reminders of yet eroding
Tides, diminishing sandbanks
On life's evermore littered shores.
Time did not flow
In ordered, conscious moments.
It fled.

VIGIL

Long night, scraped with snoring.
Keys searching for a keyhole in the corridor.
Distant engines coloring the streets,
A midnight siren plumbs the depths of sleep.
Strict amber streetlights flaring in the East,
A legion of seconds in the hall.
Misshapen questions burning on the lips,
Home memories lie heavily in mind.
A shadow spreads itself across the floor,
An abacus of action out of reach.
Charted furrows in an unwilling palm,
The magic of lamplit windows in the dark,
Cushions to ease the wear of yesteryear.
Long night, all scored with sharps.

VISIT TO THE LOUVRE

I could not tell you what you wished to know.
You went away.
A gray, uncertain day,
Flags waiting to run before a wind
Hinting daffodil promises in the park.
Dark vultures answer the crying child,
Raped by the rod of hunger.
Bring me bright gold ingots,
To stone away the crows' feet
In Van Gogh's azure sky,
Foreclosing in above the trees,
Above the terracotta-red roofs.
There, you see,
No stream of Lethe, nor ferryman's boat,
Only shuttered towers
Stretching into the gathering evening.

WORDS

You will scan these naïve lines
In an occupied, unfamiliar tomorrow,
Judas cage, built stone on stone by a
Bemused mason, pouring concrete,
Visions of power pylons in the sky.
Morning glory dreams, your eyes
Across the matrix of the swift-bleached years.
Hope, the swell of a tender calyx,
Guards a green clash of outstretched
Scimitars. Long distant voices in escrow,
Blood red telephone.

YOURS FAITHFULLY

We grow apart across the cobalt seas.
I, craving fresh winds to reflate the sails
Of old resolutions.
You, mending a torn yellow dress
In a cold November morning.
A wash of white linen
Fanfares on a fragile line.
This cat's all poised to decide.
In an ambitious leap,
Constrained by crippling fear
In the angry violet night.
Souvenirs become satire,
Absent sunlight.
Tumescence of faded forget-me-not
On the dusty cobwebbed floor.
Remorseful dawn flaring in the East.

BIRDS

Unassuming brown sparrows,
Syrinxes singing in the rain.
Darting, blue-tanned swallows,
Gold finches, sheltering yet again,
In the swaying rosemary trees.
Iridescent hummingbirds dart
Through the warm evening breeze,
Beating wings, four-chambered heart,
A veritable metabolic rate miracle.
Alert blue jay, head cocked in search,
Awaiting a meal on a twig pinnacle.
Now a red cardinal stands, wing hurt,
An august vision, unready for flight.
Hairy woodpecker tapping its trunk,
Drumming with all of its focused might.
Black-coated starling, silent as a monk,
Preparing to spread its wings again.
Ave, all warm-blooded vertebrates,
Singing and soaring, hope regained,
Daily delights, Earth's life celebrates.

APPROACHING THE ACROPOLIS

Today, intending migrants weep
Tossed in the stormy blue Aegean.
Yesterday, wily Ulysses set forth,
Surging towards the walls of Troy.
Today, the slow train from Piraeus,
Filled with tourists and tradesmen.
Yesterday, Leonidas' 300 Spartans
Fought in vain to defend Thermopylae
From Xerxes' triumphant Persian forces.
Today, curious visitors outnumber residents
In the hot and crowded streets of Athens,
All a-jostling for souvenirs and shopping.
Yesterday, the royal palace at Acropolis,
Home of Zeus, Apollo, Artemis and Aphrodite,
Citadel and fortress, looms over the city,
Today, a slow climb up the rocky crags,
A dream of Ionic pillars and Doric columns,
As an amphitheater echoes with elocution.
Yesterday, the altars of Athena's Parthenon
Welcomed worshippers and their prayers,
Destroyed then rebuilt at the urging of Pericles.
Today, the limestone rock of the high city,
Draws the gaze across thousands of years,
Construction launched in Bronze Age mists.
Yesterday's Parthenon shimmered in sunlight,
Visions of Callicrates, Phidias, and Ictinus.
Today, the Elgin Marbles stand at rest,
In the echoing halls of the British Museum.

MORNING GLORY

Blazing blue morning glory flowers,
White centers tinted with modest yellow.
Green leaves forming mourning hearts,
Burning with obsessive, unrequited love,
In the brief span of a passing day.
Pearl-white morning glory flowers,
Benign blessings, poisonous ingested.
Purple morning glory flowers,
Pink-white tunnels draw the eye.
Pale blue morning glory flowers,
Counseling strength and resilience.
Yellow-starred morning glory flowers,
Sensitive, ethereal innocence in bloom.
Radiant red morning glory flowers,
Radially symmetrical corolla, fused petals.
Contradictory *Ipomoea muricata* flowers,
Morning glories blooming at night.
Morning glory vines, shady parasols,
Alluring, hallucinogenic *Ipomoea violacea*,
Morning glory seeds of temptation.
Morning glory's lambent topaz limpidity,
Singing canticles under cerulean skies.
Morning glory's lambent, melodic memories,
If nothing lasts, every minute matters.

MIRRORS

An unblinking, appraising gaze
Reflected questions curve time.
Memories'' uncharted maze
Cautionary warnings chime.
Salt and pepper hair turning
White, eyes that sparkle no more,
And yet no cause for mourning,
At the break of each day's shore.
If a wrinkled forehead persists,
And a protesting knee resists,
An energizing privilege for each
Heart is to extend others' reach.
A long-distance run is now a dream,
Yet the wisdom of wonder, a stream,
Bearing the spirit through life's rapids,
Beyond the measurement of lipids.
Remembered achievements, inverted
Hopes and fears cloud reflection,
The passage of the years accepted,
Thoughts and habits, an accretion,
An alert, yet youthful soul reflected.

PALE BLUE DOT

Look homeward, Voyager,
Propelled by gravitational slingshots
And thermoelectric generators,
Into the dark matter and darker energy
Beyond the heliosphere, into interstellar space.
Look homeward, Voyager
Toward a world dominated by water,
Where the synergies and elegance
Of human bodies, brains and hearts
Created you, yet continue deploying
Ingrained fight-flight-freeze reactions.
All too often destroying each other,
Damaging our only home of Earth,
In its goldilocks orbit around the Sun.
Look homeward, Voyager,
Intensely packed instrumentation,
Golden record of greetings from Earth,
Oceans and waterfalls, music and drama,
Human science and art, for alien review.
Look homeward, Voyager,
Orienting thrusters, transmission radio disk,
Trained on a world where human awareness
And curiosity yet flame in dark caves,
Where we don't know what is unknown,
While the rapidly warming climate of Earth
Worsens typhoons and tornados, fires and floods.
Look homeward, Voyager,
Where the luminosity of a blue and white dot
Defines the locus of human history and hope.

www.ingramcontent.com/pod-product-compliance
Lightning Source LLC
LaVergne TN
LVHW020416070526
838199LV00054B/3626